3—

THE MUSIC TREE
ACTIVITIES

$17.99

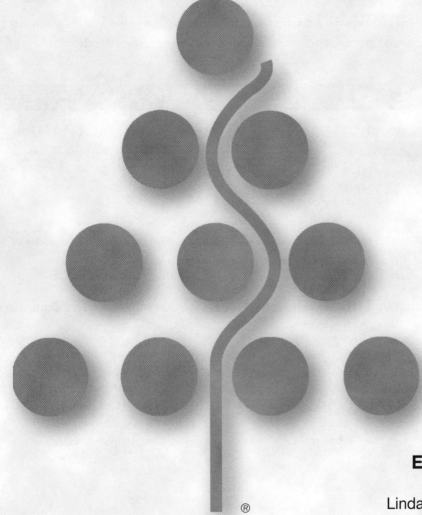

PART 3

by
Frances Clark
Louise Goss
Sam Holland
Craig Sale

D1561237

Educational Consultants:

Steve Betts	Yat Yee Chong
Linda Christensen	Ted Cooper
Amy Glennon	Monica Hochstedler
Peter Jutras	Elvina Pearce
Mary Frances Reyburn	Craig Sale

ISBN 1-58951-001-1

PREFACE

We are proud to present this latest revision of **THE MUSIC TREE,** the most carefully researched and laboratory-tested series for elementary and intermediate piano students available.

This edition combines the best of the old and the new—a natural, child-oriented sequence of learning experiences that has always been the hallmark of Frances Clark materials, combined with new music of unprecedented variety and appeal. Great pedagogy and great music—a winning combination!

The elementary section of **THE MUSIC TREE** consists of the eight books listed below, to be used in sequence. Each level has a textbook and an activities book to be used together:

TEXTBOOKS	ACTIVITIES BOOKS
TIME TO BEGIN (the primer)	**TIME TO BEGIN ACTIVITIES**
MUSIC TREE 1 (formerly A)	**ACTIVITIES 1**
MUSIC TREE 2A (formerly B)	**ACTIVITIES 2A**
MUSIC TREE 2B (formerly C)	**ACTIVITIES 2B**

Used together, these companion volumes provide a comprehensive plan for musical growth at the piano and prepare for the early intermediate materials that follow at Level 3.

The early intermediate section of **THE MUSIC TREE** (LEVEL 3) consists of five books to be used together:

THE MUSIC TREE PART 3		ACTIVITIES PART 3
KEYBOARD LITERATURE 3 An exciting new collection of gems from the 18th, 19th, and 20th centuries.	**STUDENTS' CHOICE 3** A winning collection of all-time recital favorites.	**KEYBOARD TECHNIC 3** A comprehensive new compendium of essential exercises and etudes.

We are deeply indebted to the students and faculty of The New School for Music Study and the Southern Methodist University Preparatory Department, who have been the inspiration and proving ground for this new edition, and to our educational consultants who have reviewed and tested the materials at every step of their development.

It is our hope that **THE MUSIC TREE** will provide for you the same success and delight in teaching that we have experienced, and that your students will share with ours the excitement of this new adventure in learning.

CONTENTS

UNIT ONE

Theory

Major Keys and Scales: A Review – C, G and D

Major scales are made of whole steps except for two half steps.
The half steps always come between degrees 3-4 and 7-1.

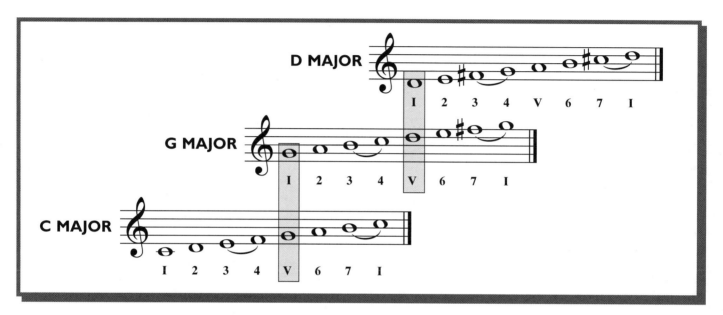

On each keyboard:
- write the name on each key
- number the degrees
- mark the two half steps

On each staff:
- write the key signature

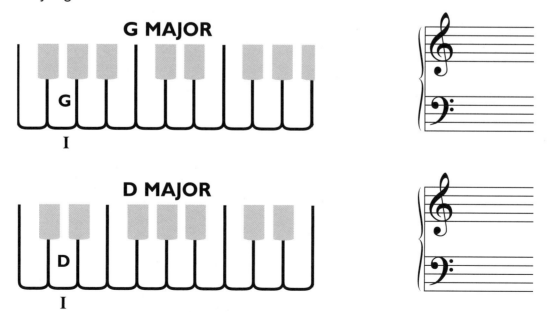

For correlated Discoveries, Repertoire and Technic see MUSIC TREE 3, pages 4-10.

4

I and *V* Triads in Major Keys

For each key signature, draw the tonic and dominant triads in both staves. Then fill in the root of each triad. The first one is done to show you how.

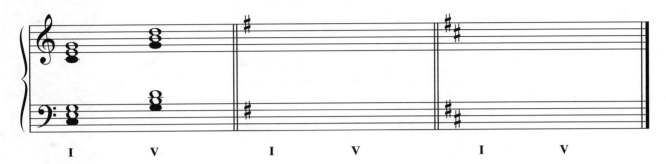

Accompanying and Transposing

In **Music Tree 2B**, you learned to accompany melodies using 5ths and 6ths.

As a review, accompany *Lavender's Blue*:
- use 5ths for parts made mostly of triad tones (degrees 1, 3, 5)
- use 6ths for parts made mostly of non-triad tones (degrees 2, 4, 6, 7)
    - sometimes raise the top note of the 5th
    - sometimes lower the bottom note of the 5th

Let your ear be your guide!

Lavender's Blue is in the key of _____ major.

Lavender's Blue

English

Now transpose *Lavender's Blue* with your accompaniment to the keys of C major and D major.

Rhythm

Learning about 16th Notes

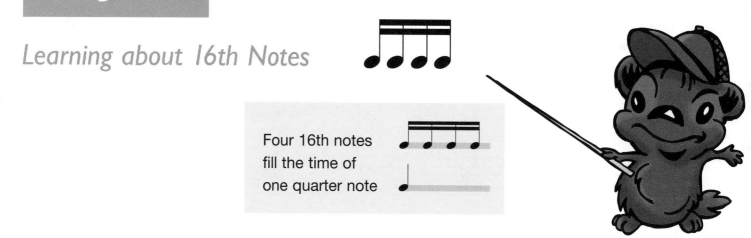

Four 16th notes
fill the time of
one quarter note

1. Swing and say the rhyme with a strong rhythmic pulse,
   one full arm swing for each pulse.

Treasure Hunt

Search - ing, search - ing   for an - oth - er clue.   If   I   find   it   I'll know what to do.

"Tick - tock   tick - tock,"   time is run - ning out.   When I find the trea - sure I will   shout!

2. Say the rhyme again, making dashes under the words –
   one dash for each pulse.

3. Then walk the rhythm as you say the rhyme,
   taking one step for each pulse.

6

Counting 16th Notes

In each of these rhythms, set a strong rhythmic pulse:

1. Point and count.

2. Tap and count.

Playing 16th Notes

Before playing each of these pieces:

1. Point and count.

2. Tap and count.

Sight-Playing

Sight-playing is playing a piece **at first sight** without practice.

Here are the steps:

1. Circle the clefs. Then prepare your hands and fingers on the correct keys.

2. Set a **slow tempo**, counting two measures out loud in a strong rhythmic pulse.

3. Play and count with a full tone, **no stopping** from beginning to end!

Arabian Magic

Evening Song

Grand Waltz

8

Crossword Puzzle

ACROSS

1.

2. Notes in the D major scale (include #'s)

3. Notes in the C major scale

4. Italian for "the end"

DOWN

5.

6. Notes in the G major scale (include #'s)

7.

8. Italian abbreviation for "to the beginning"

Theory

Inversions of Triads

Here are three different ways to spell the C major triad.
These new spellings are called INVERSIONS.

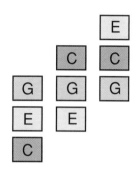

Root position   1st inversion   2nd inversion

1. Fill in the boxes to spell the inversions of each triad.
2. Draw the inversions on the staff.

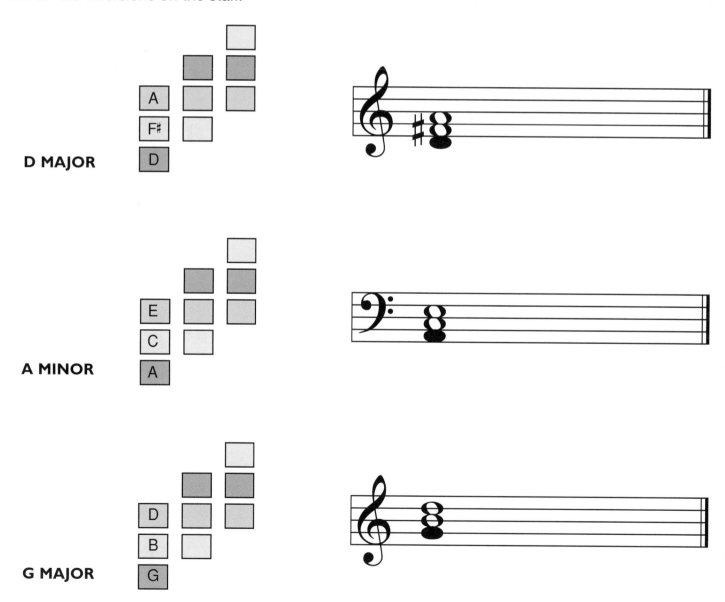

D MAJOR

A MINOR

G MAJOR

For correlated Discoveries, Repertoire and Technic see MUSIC TREE 3, pages 11-16.

Major Keys and Scales: A Review – F and B♭

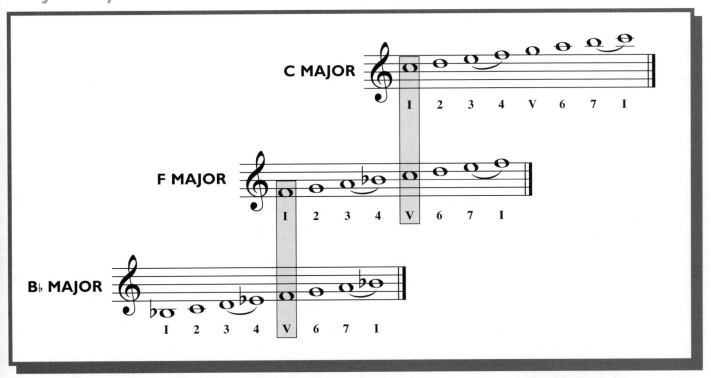

On each keyboard:
- write the name on each key
- number the degrees
- mark the two half steps

On each staff:
- write the key signature

F MAJOR

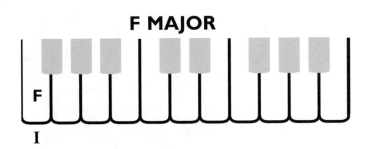

B♭ MAJOR

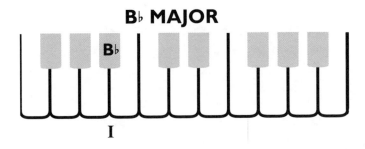

Accompanying and Transposing

Here is a melody to accompany with 5ths and **both** kinds of 6ths:

Let your ear be your guide!

For He's a Jolly Good Fellow is in the key of _____ major.

For He's a Jolly Good Fellow

Traditional

Now transpose *For He's a Jolly Good Fellow* with your accompaniment to the keys of C major and D major.

Rhythm

Counting 16th Notes

In each of these rhythms, set a strong rhythmic pulse:

1. Point and count.

2. Tap and count.

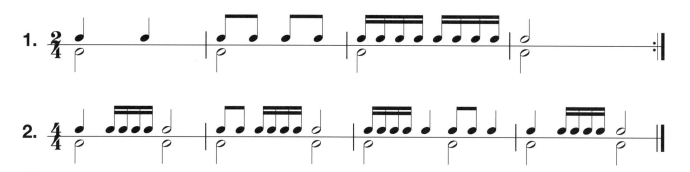

Playing 16th Notes

Before playing each of these pieces:

1. Point and count.

2. Tap and count.

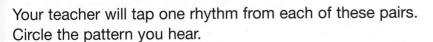

Ear Detective

Your teacher will tap one rhythm from each of these pairs.
Circle the pattern you hear.

Your teacher will play a **2nd** or a **5th**.
Circle the interval you hear.

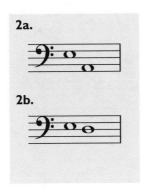

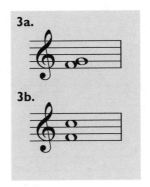

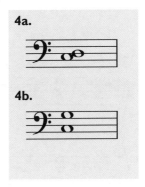

Sight-Playing

Before playing each piece, observe the key and time signatures.
Then set a strong rhythmic pulse.

Western Sunset is in the key of _____ major.

Western Sunset

Storm Warning has _____ pulses in each measure.

Storm Warning

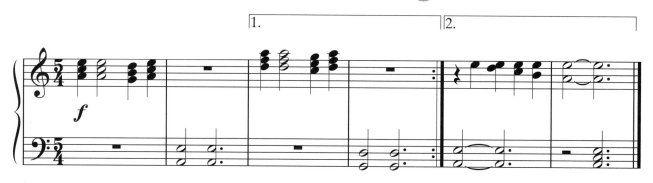

Tropical Island is in the key of _____ major.

Tropical Island

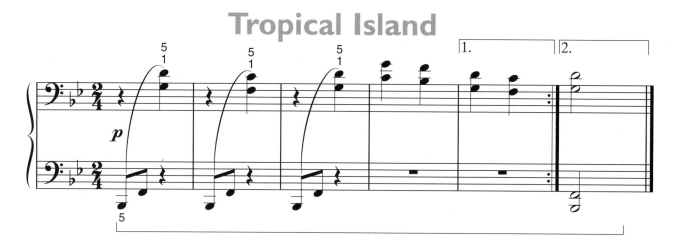

Maze

Find your way through the maze by following all the **inversions**.

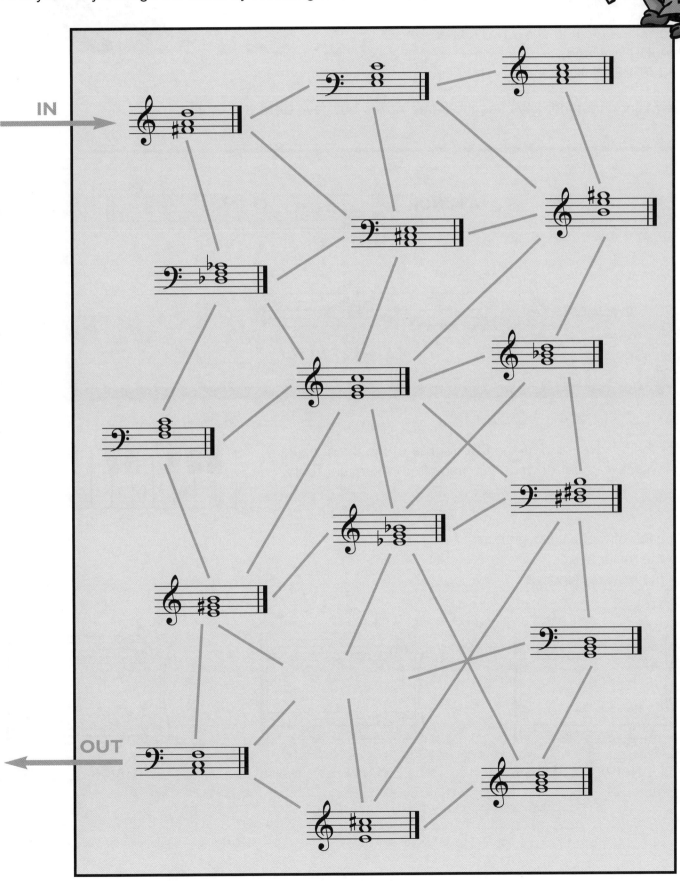

Theory

Relative Keys – C Major and A Minor

Every key signature can show two related keys:
  a MAJOR key, and
  a RELATIVE MINOR key

Relative major and minor keys use the **same notes** but have **different tonics**.

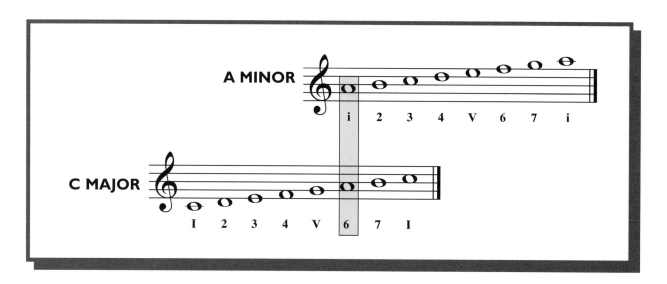

Tonic for the relative minor is the **6th degree** of the major scale.
To find it quickly, count down 3 half steps from the major tonic.

Identify each of these key signatures:
  • as the major key
  • as the relative minor key

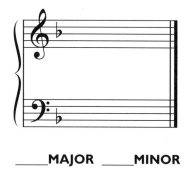

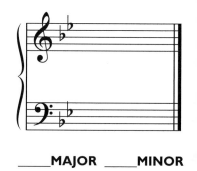

____MAJOR ____MINOR   ____MAJOR ____MINOR   ____MAJOR ____MINOR

For correlated Discoveries, Repertoire and Technic see MUSIC TREE 3, pages 17-23.

Triads and Inversions

These keyboards show the G major triad and inversions.

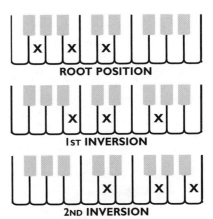

ROOT POSITION

1ST INVERSION

2ND INVERSION

On each keyboard, mark the triad tones and circle the root.
Then write the triad and inversions on the staff.
The first example is started to show you how.

D MAJOR

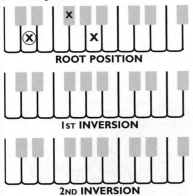

ROOT POSITION

1ST INVERSION

2ND INVERSION

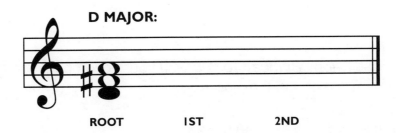

D MAJOR:

ROOT   1ST   2ND

F MAJOR:

ROOT   1ST   2ND

F MAJOR

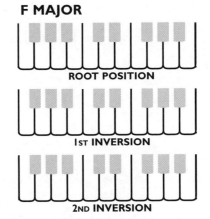

ROOT POSITION

1ST INVERSION

2ND INVERSION

A MINOR

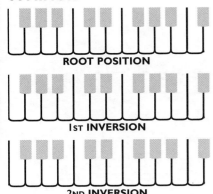

ROOT POSITION

1ST INVERSION

2ND INVERSION

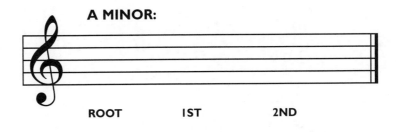

A MINOR:

ROOT   1ST   2ND

Accompanying and Transposing

Here is a melody to accompany with 5ths and **both** kinds of 6ths:
Let your ear be your guide!

Happy Birthday To You is in the key of _____ major.

Happy Birthday To You

Hill and Hill

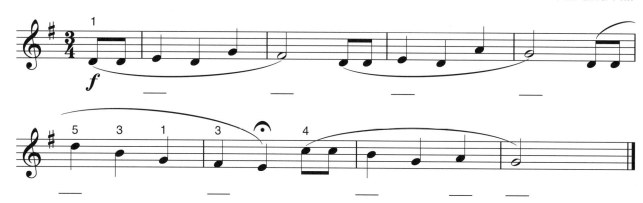

Now transpose *Happy Birthday To You* with your accompaniment
to the keys of C major and F major.

Ear Detective

Your teacher will tap one rhythm from each of these pairs.
Circle the pattern you hear.

Your teacher will play a **2nd**, **3rd** or **5th**.
Circle the interval you hear.

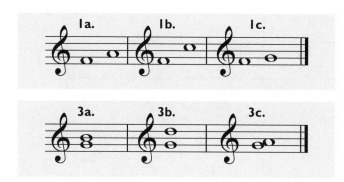

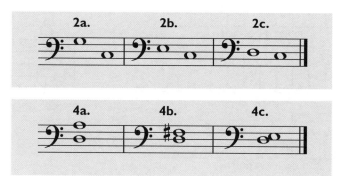

Rhythm

Crazy Rhythms

In each of the rhythms below:
1. Point and count.
2. Tap and count.
3. Tap, clap, snap and count.

♩ = TAP   ♩ = CLAP your hands   ♩ = SNAP your fingers

Set a slow and steady tempo. When secure, try it faster.

1.

2.

Rhythm Detective

Write the time signature for each rhythm in the box provided.

1.

2.

Add measure bars and ending bar to each of these rhythms.

1.

2.

Sight-Playing

Before playing each piece, observe the key and time signatures.
Then set a strong rhythmic pulse.

At the Races is in the key of _____ major.

At the Races

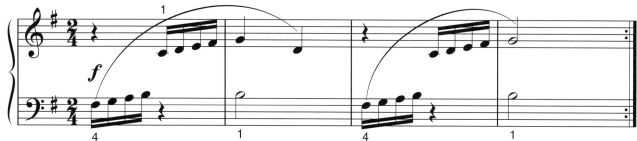

Russian Dance is in the key of _____ minor.

Russian Dance

Tumbling is in the key of _____ major.

Tumbling

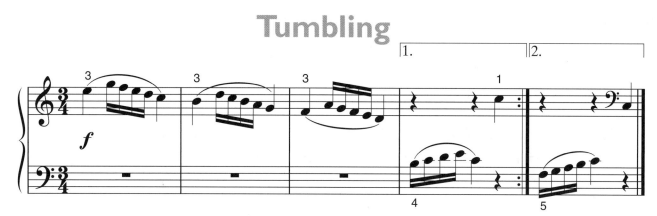

Rhythm Puzzle

Below are the rhythms of a well-known melody in compound meter.
Tap and count each box and see if you can unscramble the rhythm.
Copy the measures in the correct order.

The picture provides a clue!

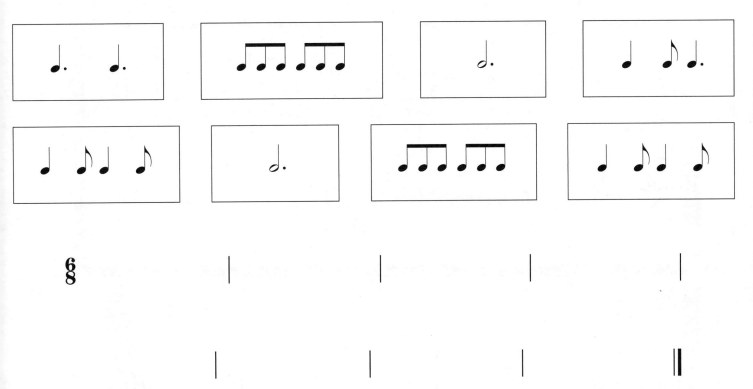

What is the name of the melody? _____

Theory

Relative Keys — F Major and D Minor

F major and D minor are relative keys.
The key of D minor is built on the **6th degree** of F major.

In minor keys, the dominant triad is usually a major triad.
In order to make the dominant triad major, the 7th scale degree is raised *one half step*.

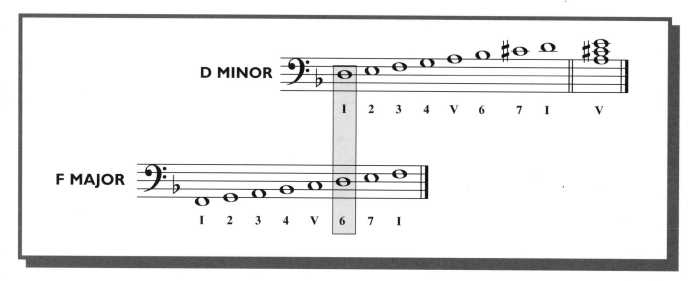

I and *V* Triads in Minor Keys

For each minor scale:
- raise the 7th degree of the scale by drawing a sharp
- write the dominant triad in the blank measure
- add a sharp to make the dominant triad major

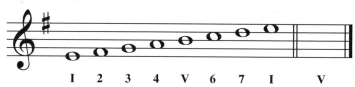

For correlated Discoveries, Repertoire and Technic see MUSIC TREE 3, pages 24-30.

Major or Minor?

Before playing this melody, answer these questions:

What two keys does the key signature show? _____ major _____ minor

Do the first and last notes of the melody belong to the tonic triad
of the major or minor key?   MAJOR   MINOR

Is the 7th degree of the minor scale raised?   YES   NO

So, this melody is in the key of: C MAJOR   A MINOR

Accompanying and Transposing

Tarantella is in the key of _____ minor.
When you can play it easily, accompany it with 5ths and 6ths.
Use the raised 7th degree when playing 6ths that move the **bottom** note.

Tarantella

Italian

Now transpose *Tarantella* with your accompaniment to the key of D minor.

Rhythm

Counting "Swing" Rhythms

In each of these rhythms, set a strong rhythmic pulse:

1. Tap and count with even eighth notes.

2. Tap and count in "swing" style.

Playing "Swing" Rhythms

Before playing each of these pieces in "swing" style:

1. Tap and count with even eighth notes.

2. Tap and count in "swing" style.

Rhythm Detective

Find and circle the measures that have too few pulses.

Ear Detective

Your teacher will tap one rhythm from each of these pairs.
Circle the pattern you hear.

Your teacher will play either a **2nd** or a **4th**.
Circle the interval you hear.

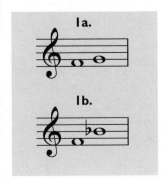

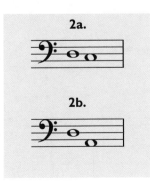

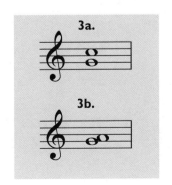

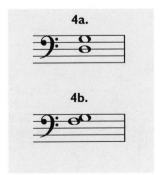

Sight-Playing

Before playing each piece, observe the key and time signatures.
Then set a strong rhythmic pulse.

Dance in 16ths is in the key of _____ major.

Dance in 16ths

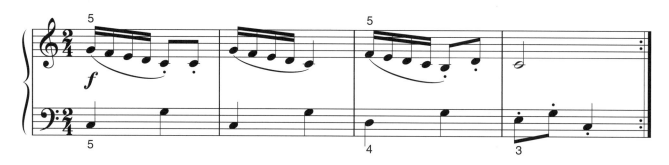

Seascape is in the key of _____ minor.

Seascape

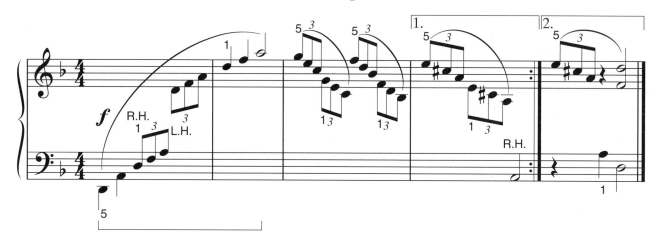

Crab Dance is in the key of _____ minor.

Crab Dance

Puzzling Triads

Spell each triad or inversion.
Write the letters in the boxes provided.
Then use the circled letters to complete the phrase at the bottom of the page.

1.
G major root position

2.
C major 1st inversion

3.
A major root position

4.
G major 1st inversion

5.
E minor root position

6.
A minor 2nd inversion

7.
B-flat major 1st inversion

8.
G major 2nd inversion

9.
A major 1st inversion

10.
C major 2nd inversion

Remember these words of advice when practicing triads and inversions:

____ ____ SUR ____ TO O ____ S ____ RV ____ ____ IN ____ ____ RIN ____ .

I   2   3   4   5   6   7   8 9   10

Theory

Subdominant (*IV*)

Subdominant (**IV**) is the name for degree 4 of a major or minor scale.

In the key of C major:
I is _____
IV is _____
V is _____

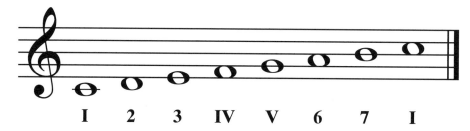

I   2   3   IV   V   6   7   I

Name the **I**, **IV** and **V** for each of these keys:

D Major   **I** is ____   **IV** is ____   **V** is ____

F Major   **I** is ____   **IV** is ____   **V** is ____

A minor   **I** is ____   **IV** is ____   **V** is ____

G Major   **I** is ____   **IV** is ____   **V** is ____

I, *IV* and *V* Triads

For each major key signature, draw the tonic, subdominant and dominant triads in both staves.

The first one is done to show you how.

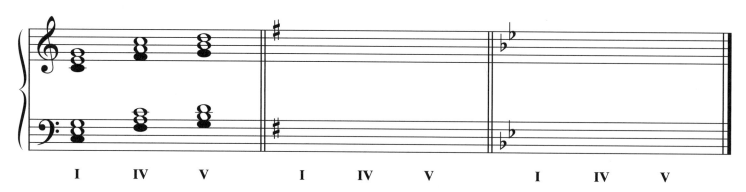

I   IV   V   I   IV   V   I   IV   V

For correlated Discoveries, Repertoire and Technic see MUSIC TREE 3, pages 31-37.

Accompanying and Transposing

Here is a melody to accompany with 5ths and 6ths:
- for parts made mostly of **I** triad tones, use 5ths
- for parts made mostly of **IV** triad tones, use 6ths (raise the top note)
- for parts made mostly of **V** triad tones, use 6ths (lower the bottom note)

Air is in the key of _____ major.

Air

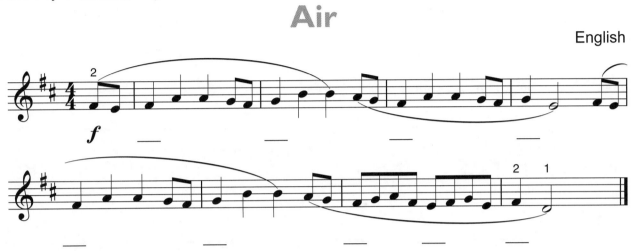

English

Now transpose *Air* with your accompaniment to the keys of B-flat major and G major.

Relative Keys – G Major and E Minor

G major and E minor are relative keys.
The key of E minor is built on the **6th degree** of G major.

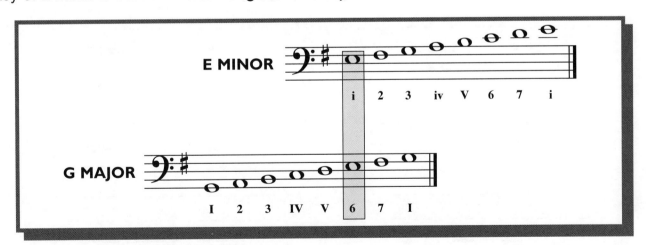

Draw the E minor scale:
- raise the 7th degree of the scale by drawing a sharp
- write the dominant triad in the blank measure
- add a sharp to make the dominant triad major

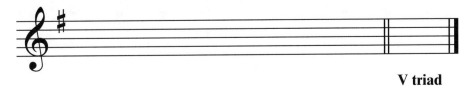

V triad

29

Rhythm

Crazy Rhythms

In each of the rhythms:

    1. Tap and count each hand alone.

    2. Tap and count hands together.

♩ = TAP on keyboard cover

✗ = TAP your head

Set a slow steady tempo. When secure, try it faster!

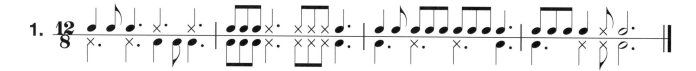

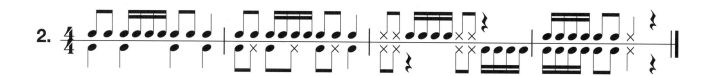

Matching

Draw a line to connect the boxes that have the same number of pulses.

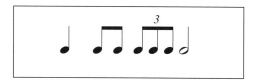

Rhythm Detective

Complete each incomplete measure with one note.

1.

2.

3.

Ear Detective

Your teacher will play a phrase using either swing or even .
Circle the style you hear.

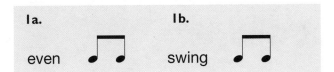

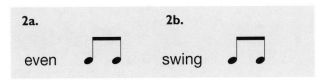

Your teacher will play a **2nd**, **3rd**, **4th** or **5th**.
Circle the interval you hear.

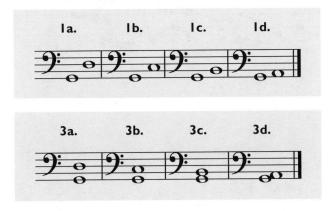

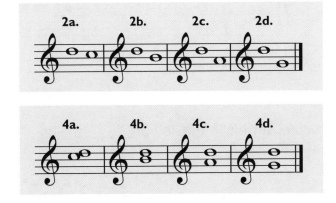

Your teacher will play a chord progression using **I**, **IV** and **V**.
Circle the progression you hear.

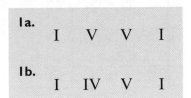

1a.   I   V   V   I

1b.   I   IV   V   I

2a.   I   I   V   I

2b.   I   V   IV   I

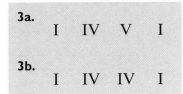

3a.   I   IV   V   I

3b.   I   IV   IV   I

31

Sight-Playing

Before playing each piece, observe the key and time signatures.
Then set a strong rhythmic pulse.

Swingin' is in the key of _____ major.

Swingin'

Goblins and Ghosts is in the key of _____ minor.

Goblins and Ghosts

Staccato Strut is in the key of _____ major.

Staccato Strut

Word Search

Circle the word that corresponds to each symbol or clue.
The word may go forward, up, down or diagonally.

1. **IV**

2. **I** 2 3 **IV V** 6 7 **I**

3. C major & A minor

4. relative key of G major

5. relative key of F major

6. ♪♪♪♪

7. 𝄢 8/8 8/8

8. **I**

9. **V**

10. *f*

S	Z	A	Y	E	F	O	R	T	E	C
E	U	U	E	M	T	R	F	S	G	Q
T	R	B	H	I	Q	E	I	P	J	M
O	O	K	D	N	N	L	L	M	Y	G
N	Z	A	O	O	B	A	V	W	C	O
H	D	T	M	R	M	T	U	E	F	Z
T	R	S	I	D	M	I	N	O	R	N
N	G	H	N	P	Q	V	N	I	C	T
E	J	N	A	O	K	E	L	A	I	M
E	M	A	N	C	B	K	D	C	N	K
T	G	F	T	H	G	E	I	H	O	T
X	J	L	N	P	R	Y	T	V	T	W
I	M	A	J	O	R	S	C	A	L	E
S	I	N	V	E	R	S	I	O	N	S

UNIT SIX

Theory

Accompanying Using Triads and Inversions

Tonic, subdominant and dominant triads can be used to accompany melodies.

 Tonic (root position) accompanies parts made mostly of **I** triad tones

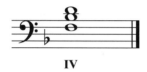 Subdominant (2nd inversion) accompanies parts made mostly of **IV** triad tones

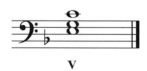 Dominant (1st inversion) accompanies parts made mostly of **V** triad tones

Twinkle, Twinkle Little Star is in the key of _____ major.

I is _____. **IV** is _____. **V** is _____.

Twinkle, Twinkle Little Star

French

Now transpose *Twinkle, Twinkle Little Star* with your accompaniment to the keys of C and D major.

For correlated Discoveries, Repertoire and Technic see MUSIC TREE 3, pages 38-42.

34

Identifying Triads and Inversions

Draw a line to connect each chord to the correct label.

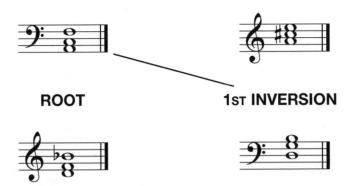

ROOT　　　　　　**1ST INVERSION**　　　　　　**2ND INVERSION**

Finding the Roots of Triads

The root of a triad in root position is the bottom note.

ROOT

To find the root of an inverted triad:
- find the interval of a 4th
- the top note of the 4th is the root of the triad

1st inv.　　　**2nd inv.**

For each triad:
- fill in the root
- write the name of the root

1.

G

2.

_____

3.

_____

4.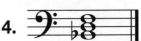

_____

5.

_____

6.

_____

35

Rhythm

Learning about

Two 16th notes
last as long as
one eighth note.

1. Swing and say the rhyme with a strong rhythmic pulse,
   one full arm swing for each pulse.

Sing a Song of Sixpence

Sing a song of six-pence, pock-et full of rye,

Four and twen-ty black-birds, baked in a pie.

When the pie was o-pened, the birds be-gan to sing!

Was-n't that a dain-ty dish to set be-fore the king?

2. Say the rhyme again, making dashes under the words –
   one dash for each pulse:

3. Then, walk the rhythm as you say the rhyme,
   taking one step for each pulse.

Counting

In each of these rhythms, set a strong rhythmic pulse:

1. Point and count.

2. Tap and count.

Playing

Before playing each of these pieces:

1. Point and count.

2. Tap and count.

Sight-Playing

Before playing each piece, observe the key and time signatures.
Then set a strong rhythmic pulse.

Yodeling is in the key of _____ major.

Yodeling

Penguins is in the key of _____ major.

Penguins

Music Box is in the key of _____ major.

Music Box

Crossword Puzzle

ACROSS

1. F major (2nd inversion)

2.

3. ♫ = ♩♪
   ⌐3¬

4. Subdominant

5. 𝄐

DOWN

3. Raised scale degree in minor scales

6. F major's "relative"

7. C major's "relative"

8. E minor's "relative"

9. Dance in 3/4

10. F major (root position)

Theory

Interval Inversions

When an interval is inverted, a different interval is created.
When a 2nd is inverted, it becomes a 7th; a 3rd becomes a 6th;
a 4th becomes a 5th; and so on.

Complete these examples by drawing and identifying the inversion of each interval.

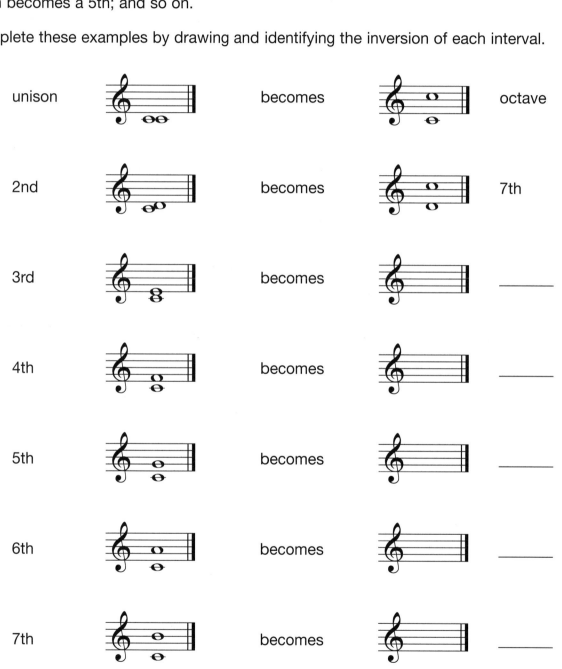

For correlated Discoveries, Repertoire and Technic see MUSIC TREE 3, pages 43-49.

Accompanying and Transposing Using **I** *and* **V7**

A dominant seventh (**V7**) is often used instead of a **V** triad.

Use the **V7** with the inverted 7th to accompany this melody.

Pawpaw Patch is in the key of _____ major.

Pawpaw Patch

Now transpose *Pawpaw Patch* with your accompaniment to the keys of F, D and B-flat major.

Ear Detective

Your teacher will tap the rhythms below. Some measures are incomplete.
Write the missing rhythm you hear.

Your teacher will play a chord progression using **I**, **IV** and **V**.
Circle the progression you hear.

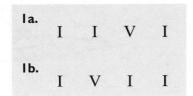

la.			
I	I	V	I

lb.			
I	V	I	I

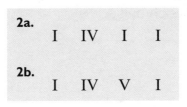

2a.			
I	IV	I	I

2b.			
I	IV	V	I

Rhythm

Learning about Syncopation

Syncopation is a shift in rhythmic emphasis from a
strong part of the pulse to a part that is normally weaker.

A common form of syncopation is:

It is usually written:

1. Swing and say the rhyme with a strong rhythmic pulse.

Bill Bailey

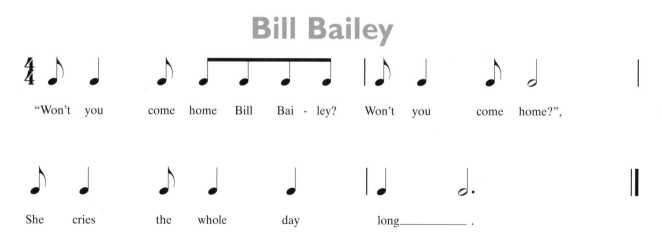

2. Say the rhyme again making dashes under the words –
   one dash for each pulse:

3. Then walk the rhythm as you say the rhyme,
   taking one step for each pulse.

42

Counting Syncopation

In each of these rhythms, set a strong rhythmic pulse:

1. Point and count.

2. Tap and count.

Playing Syncopation

Before playing each of these pieces:

1. Point and count.

2. Tap and count.

Latin Swing

Jazz Waltz

Sight-Playing

Before playing each piece, observe the key and time signatures.
Then set a strong rhythmic pulse.

Making Progress is in the key of _____ major.

Making Progress

Workmen's Song is in the key of _____ minor.

Workmen's Song

In the Park is in the key of _____ major.

In the Park

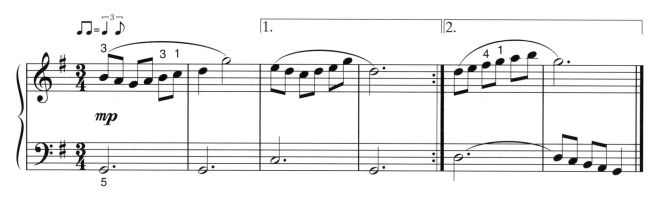

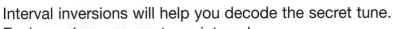

Secret Tune

Interval inversions will help you decode the secret tune.
Each number represents an interval.

On the line below each number, write the number of the interval's inversion.
This number is the scale degree used in the tune.
Write this note on the staff using the rhythm shown.
Then, accompany the melody with **I** and **V7**.

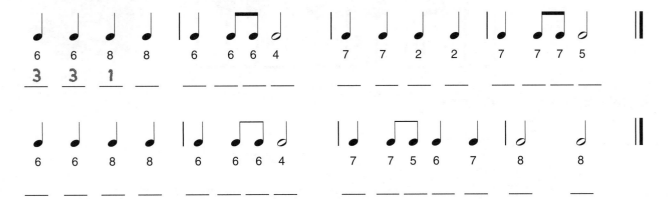

(Write the name of the tune)

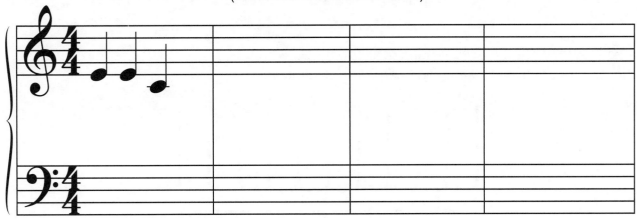

Theory

Chromatic Scales

Chromatic scales are made entirely of half steps.
They can begin or end on any note.
They use every key, white and black, in order.

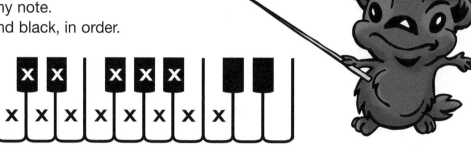

On the staff, chromatic scales use:

sharps as they go **up**

flats as they go **down**

On this keyboard, write the C chromatic scale going UP.
• write the name on each key (use sharps for black keys)

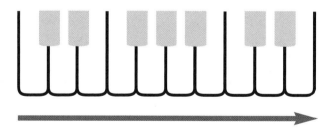

On this keyboard, write the C chromatic scale going DOWN.
• write the name on each key (use flats for black keys)

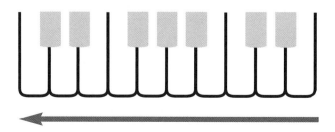

For correlated Discoveries, Repertoire and Technic see MUSIC TREE 3, pages 50-55.

Accompanying and Transposing Using *I, IV* and *V7*

Accompany this melody with **I**, **IV** and **V7**.
- for parts made mostly of **I** triad tones use **I**
- for parts made mostly of **IV** triad tones use **IV**
- for parts made mostly of **V** triad tones use **V7**

This Little Light of Mine is in the key of _____ major.

I is _____.   **IV** is _____.   **V** is _____.

This Little Light of Mine

Traditional

Now transpose *This Little Light of Mine* with your accompaniment to the keys of G major and F major.

Ear Detective

Your teacher will play chord progressions using either **V** or **V7**.
Circle the progression that you hear.

1a. I IV V I	**2a.** I V7 V7 I	**3a.** I V IV V I
1b. I IV V7 I	**2b.** I V V I	**3b.** I V7 IV V7 I

Your teacher will play either a **2nd**, **3rd**, **4th** or **5th** above the notes given.
- • Label the interval in the space below.
- • Write the second note on the staff.

Rhythm

Counting Syncopation

In each of these rhythms, set a strong rhythmic pulse:

1. Point and count the harder part.

2. Tap and count hands together.

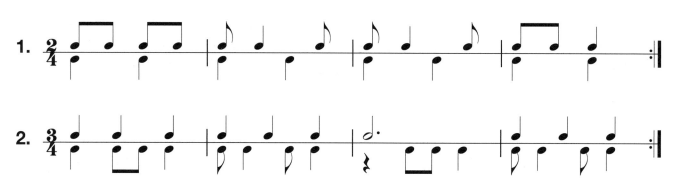

Rhythm Detective

Complete each incomplete measure with one note.

Sight-Playing

Before playing each piece, observe the key and time signatures.
Then set a strong rhythmic pulse.

Fanfare is in the key of _____ major.

Fanfare

Mississippi Blues is in the key of _____ major.

Mississippi Blues

Desert Caravan is in the key of _____ minor.

Desert Caravan

Syncopation Maze

Find your way through the maze by following the syncopated patterns that have four quarter note pulses.

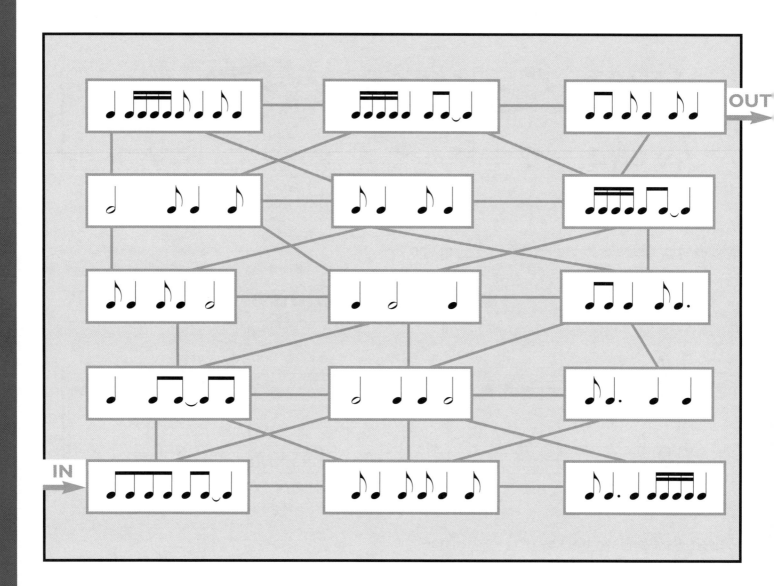

Now tap and count your way through the maze non-stop.

Theory

Whole-Tone Scales

Whole-tone scales are made entirely of whole steps.
Like chromatic scales, they can begin on any note.

C WHOLE-TONE SCALE

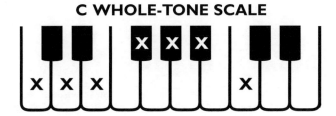

C# WHOLE-TONE SCALE

On the staff, whole-tone scales use:

sharps as they go **up**

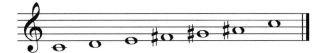

flats as they go **down**

On this keyboard, write the C# whole-tone scale going UP.
• write the name on each key (use sharps for black keys)

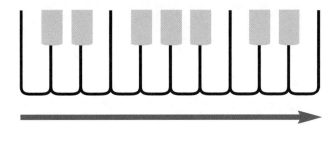

On this keyboard, write the D♭ whole-tone scale going DOWN.
• write the name on each key (use flats for black keys)

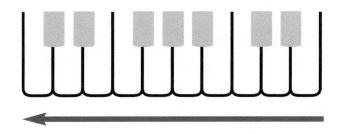

For correlated Discoveries, Repertoire and Technic see MUSIC TREE 3, pages 56-60.

Accompanying and Transposing Using **I**, **IV** *and* **V7**

Accompany this melody with **I**, **IV** and **V7**.
- for parts made mostly of **I** triad tones use **I**
- for parts made mostly of **IV** triad tones use **IV**
- for parts made mostly of **V** triad tones use **V7**

The Lion Sleeps Tonight is in the key of _____ major.

I is _____.   **IV** is _____.   **V** is _____.

The Lion Sleeps Tonight

New lyric and revised music by
George David Weiss, Hugo Peretti and Luigi Creatore

Now transpose *The Lion Sleeps Tonight* with your accompaniment to the keys of C and B-flat major.

Ear Detective

Your teacher will play chord progressions using either **I**, **IV** and **V7**.
Fill in the missing chords.

1. **I**   **IV**   ____   ____   2. **I**   ____   ____   **I**

3. **I**   ____   ____   **I**   4. **IV**   **I**   ____   **I**

Your teacher will play a **2nd**, **3rd**, **4th** or **5th** above the notes given.
   Label the interval in the space below.
   Write the second note on the staff.

Your teacher will tap the rhythms below. Some measures are incomplete.
Write the missing rhythm that you hear.

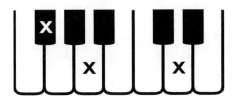 

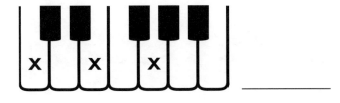 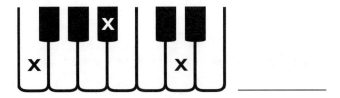

Triads and Inversions

Identify the triad and inversion shown on each keyboard below.

D Major
1st inversion

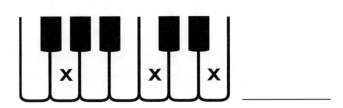

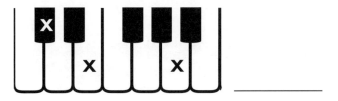

Rhythm

Crazy Rhythms

In each of these rhythms, set a strong rhythmic pulse:

1. Tap and count.

2. Tap, snap, clap and count.   = TAP    = CLAP your hands    = SNAP your fingers

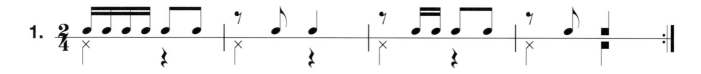

Rhythm Jumble

Circle the rhythms that have four quarter-note pulses.
  Write them in any order in the blank measures below.
  Clap and count the rhythm you created.

$\frac{4}{4}$ | | | ‖

Sight-Playing

Before playing each piece, observe the key and time signatures.
Then set a strong rhythmic pulse.

Whitewater Rafting is in the key of _____ minor.

Whitewater Rafting

Sunrise is in the key of _____ major.

Sunrise

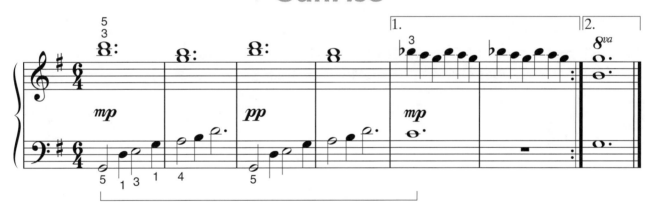

Blue Calypso is in the key of _____ major.

Blue Calypso

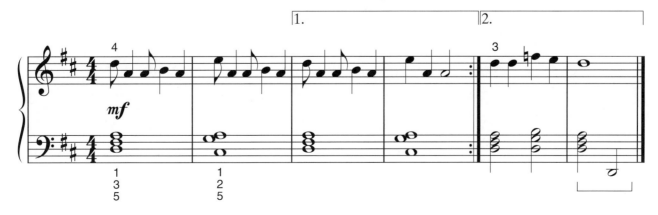

Scale Chains

1. For each part that goes UP write WHOLE TONE SCALES (using sharps).
   For each part that goes DOWN write CHROMATIC SCALES (using flats).

   The last letter of one answer becomes the first letter of the next.

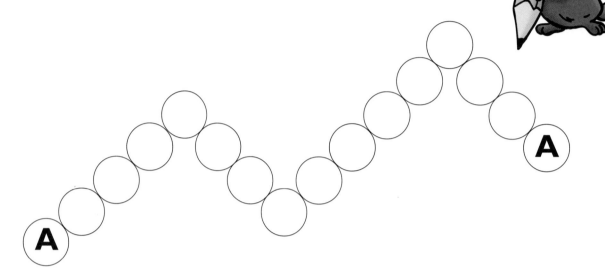

2. For each part that goes DOWN write WHOLE TONE SCALES (using flats).
   For each part that goes UP write CHROMATIC SCALES (using sharps).

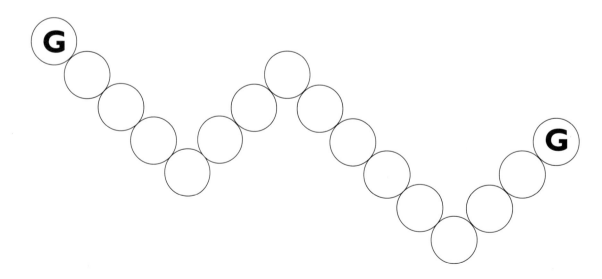

UNIT TEN

Theory

Chromatic and Whole-Tone Scales

Write the missing notes in each scale.

Chromatic scale (ascending)

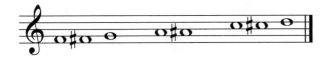

Whole-tone scale (ascending)

Chromatic scale (descending)

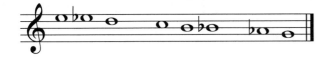

Whole-tone scale (descending)

Accompanying and Transposing Using I, IV and $V7$

To accompany this melody, follow the directions on page 52.

Old Folks at Home is in the key of _____ major.

I is _____. IV is _____. V is _____.

Old Folks at Home

Foster

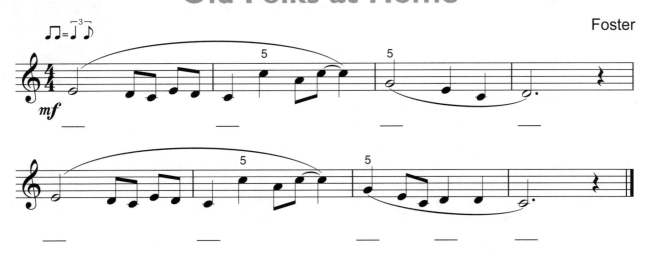

Now transpose *Old Folks at Home* with your accompaniment to the keys of G and D major.

For correlated Discoveries, Repertoire and Technic see MUSIC TREE 3, pages 61-64.

Ear Detective

Your teacher will tap the following rhythms. Some measures are blank.
Write the rhythm you hear in the blank measures.

1. $\frac{6}{8}$ ♩ ♪♩. | ‖   2. $\frac{4}{4}$ ♩ ♩ ♫♩ | ‖

3. $\frac{3}{4}$ ♩ ♫♩ | ‖   4. $\frac{4}{4}$ ♩ ♫♫♩ | ‖

Your teacher will play either a **whole-tone** or a **chromatic** scale.
Circle the one that you hear.

1a. whole tone	**2a.** whole tone	**3a.** whole tone
1b. chromatic	**2b.** chromatic	**3b.** chromatic

Your teacher will play a chord progression using **I**, **IV** and **V7**.
Fill in the missing chords.

1. **I**   **IV**   ___   **I**   2. **I**   ___   ___   **I**

3. **I**   **V7**   ___   **I**   4. **I**   **V7**   ___   **I**

Your teacher will play the following examples that use pedal.
Circle the example with the correct pedal markings.

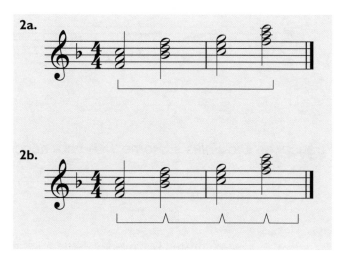

58

Rhythm

Crazy Rhythms

In each of these rhythms:

  1. Point and count.
  2. Tap, snap, clap and count.

♩ = TAP   ♩ = CLAP your hands   ✗ = SNAP your fingers

1.

2.

Rhythm Jumble

Circle the rhythms that have three quarter-note pulses.
  Write them in any order in the blank measures below.
  Clap and count the rhythm you created.

 |　　　　　|　　　　　|　　　　　‖

Sight-Playing

Before playing each piece, observe the key and time signatures.
Then set a strong rhythmic pulse.

Easy Street is in the key of _____ major.

Easy Street

Squirrels at Play is in the key of _____ major.

Squirrels at Play

Blues is in the key of _____ major.

Blues

Crossword Puzzle

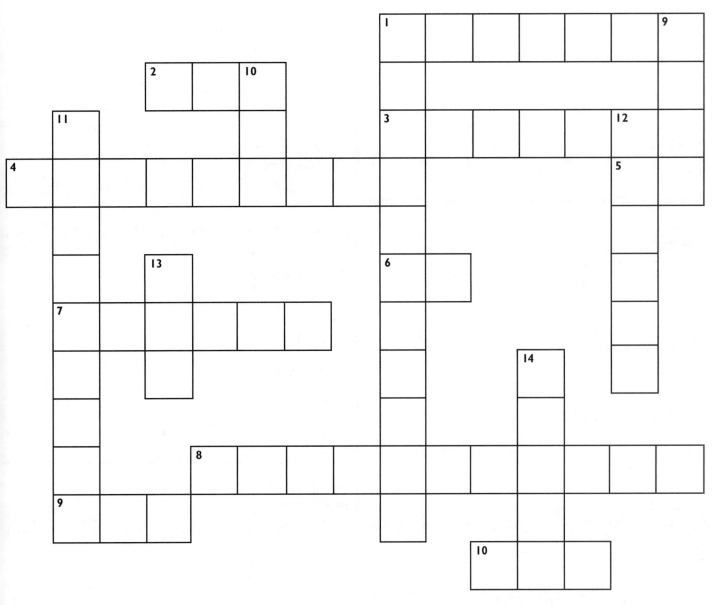

ACROSS

1. An inverted 2nd

2. F major triad in root position

3. ♮

4. Scale made entirely of half steps

5. Medium loud

6. Very soft

7.  equals this

8. **IV**

9. C major triad in 1st inversion

10. A minor triad in root position

DOWN

1. ♩ ♩ ♪ ♩ ♪

9. Step between degrees 3-4 and 7-8 in major scales

10. F major triad in 2nd inversion

11. Scale made entirely of whole steps

12. Relative key of C major

13. G major 2nd inversion

14. **I**

EAR DETECTIVE TEACHER'S KEY

Glossary

four 16th notes	♬♬	Fill the time of one quarter note
two 16th notes	♬	Fill the time of one eighth note
"swing" rhythm	♬ = ♩♪ (³)	Two eighth notes are played unevenly as if they were the first and third notes of a triplet
syncopation	♪♩ ♪	A shift in rhythmic emphasis from a strong part of the pulse to a part that is normally weaker
canon		Musical form in which one voice imitates another throughout
chromatic scale		Scale made entirely of half steps
dominant triad		Triad built on the fifth degree of any major or minor scale
dominant seventh	V7	Often used instead of a dominant triad in accompaniments
1st inversion		When the third of the triad is the bottom note of the chord
inversion		The rearrangement of the notes of a triad or interval
key signature		The sharps or flats appearing at the beginning of each staff to indicate the major or minor key of a composition
major scale		Eight tones arranged in alphabetical order; made of whole steps except for half steps between degrees 3-4 and 7-1
minor scale		Scale made of whole steps except for half steps between degrees 2-3 and 5-6; degree 7 is often raised one half step higher
minuet		Graceful dance in 3/4, common in Classical music
relative keys		A major and minor key that share the same key signature; tonic for the relative minor is the 6th degree of the major scale

Term	Symbol/Notation	Definition
root position		When the root of the triad is the bottom note of the chord
2nd inversion		When the fifth of the triad is the bottom note of the chord
subdominant	IV	The fourth degree of any major or minor scale
subdominant triad		Triad built on the fourth degree of any major or minor scale
12-bar blues		Popular musical form using **I**, **IV** and **V** chords
whole-tone scale		Scale made entirely of whole steps
		C major key signature A minor key signature
		G major key signature E minor key signature
		F major key signature D minor key signature
		D major key signature B minor key signature
		B♭ major key signature G minor key signature